C000100924

CALL
WORSHIP

A practical guide for those
involved in leading worship

MARTIN JONES

Published by
Hullo Creative Ltd.
info@hullocreative.com
www.hullocreative.com

Cover design by
Suzi Hull of Hullo Creative Ltd.

ISBN-13: 978-0-9935366-0-1

DEDICATION

This book is dedicated to all sincere lovers of God and to all passionate pursuers of His presence. As you seek Him and encounter His presence in the secret place, may you draw others into that place of intimacy as you lead them in times of corporate worship.

CONTENTS

ACKNOWLEDGMENTS

I want to especially thank **Simon Ponsonby** for inspiring me to write this book and for his continued support and encouragement and **Ben Mears** for his invaluable help in guiding me through the publishing process.

PREFACE

It has been my opinion for quite some time now that there is a real need for a brief handbook to be available to help Christians who are either just getting involved in the worship ministry, or, who are already involved and would appreciate a little help and encouragement. This book has been written especially for such people; both individuals and worship groups. It is intentionally practical and my hope is that the information contained in this book will assist you in fulfilling God's call on your life concerning the facilitating of worship, thereby bringing glory to Him.

Although much of the material in this book was compiled in the 1990's and therefore contains references to the worship genre of that time, the principles and priorities outlined regarding the leading of God's people in worship are timeless and still hold true for today.

FOREWORD

Some of my most precious memories of meeting God have Martin Jones in the frame. As a young Christian stepping out into ministry, Martin was there: leading worship at church or small groups, driving me to evangelistic events or church youth clubs where he would play performance songs and I would preach. They were great times traced with glory. Martin was hungry for the Lord, he made me want more of God and his gifting enabled me to receive more of God.

Martin even gave me my first guitar and taught me my first chords. I never graduated in the school of worship leading, but through countless hours, some very dark, Martin's guitar and the chords he taught helped me meet the Lord. Twenty Five years later, I still own scraps of paper of worship songs and chords that Martin used to help teach me.

Martin is a man of genuine humility that gives him a profound sensitivity to the Holy Spirit. A man whose soul bears life's scars which enable a genuine empathy to the human spirit.

Through his gift of worship leading he brings connection between the Holy Spirit and the human spirit. Over the past twenty-five years of ministry and the more recent privilege of wider service, I have ministered alongside the good and the great, the famed songwriters and named worship leaders of our generation. But the meek spirit of Martin that hosts the anointing of God, that I once took for granted, is rarer than it should be.

Martin, in his new book, gets out of the way and makes much of Jesus. It can be read in an afternoon, but it takes thousands of afternoons to distill such lessons. Spiritual truths underpin this practical guide - as useful for worship teams and worship leaders as for worshippers. It's a little gem. Thank you Martin, for the book, and for my guitar, and for making Jesus nearer and dearer to me.

Simon Ponsonby
Pastor of Theology
St Aldates
Oxford

CHAPTER 1

Introduction

Martin who? Martin Jones? Never heard of him! What can I learn from someone of whom I have never heard?

These are questions that you may well be asking yourself and they are not dissimilar to the concerns that I had when it was suggested by a friend of mine, Simon Ponsonby, that God might be calling me to embark on the writing of this book. Who am I to seek to instruct anyone concerning the practicalities of leading others in the worship of God?

I could sometimes relate to the person who said he was so insignificant that even his best friends had never heard of him! (I'm only kidding).

Nevertheless, I do believe that God has inspired me to write this book in order that others may benefit from the things that I have learnt, gleaned and experienced in this ministry, and ultimately so that He will be given the glory.

Many times during the writing of this book, I have entertained doubts concerning my ability to offer any fresh insights into the worship ministry that have not already been shared by those with a much higher profile than myself. But God has been faithful in sustaining me during these 'low' points.

He has continued to provide the encouragement, resources and the enthusiasm that have enabled me to persevere.

During one such period of doubting, God spoke to me through the story of the feeding of the five thousand, (Mark 6:30-44).

It was late in the day and the disciples came and shared their concerns with Jesus regarding the people's well-being. They suggested to Jesus that He should send the people away so that they could go to the surrounding countryside and villages in order to buy something to eat. Jesus' reply was unexpected: "*You* give them something to eat."

The disciples had recognised the need and brought it to the attention of Jesus expecting the local merchants to be the means used to meet that need, (verse 36). But Jesus said in essence, "*You* meet the need." Jesus didn't use the obvious channels of provision; instead the disciples were to be the answer to their own prayer and concern.

Immediately the disciples looked to their own limited resources stating that they had insufficient funds to meet the needs of the crowd, (verse 37b). But they had seriously underestimated Jesus' ability to meet the need.

God Doesn't Call the Equipped; He Equips the Called.
Jesus instructed them to use the resources available; five
loaves and two fish. He then blessed the food and
multiplied it so that everyone was satisfied. Two things
spoke to me as I meditated on these verses.

Firstly, as I have shared my concerns with God regarding
the need for more people to be enabled and equipped to
lead others in the worship of Him, He seems to be saying
to me, "You do it, using the resources that are available.
Consecrate them to Me and I will bless them and multiply
them." This has been my experience as I have
endeavoured to be faithful to the Spirit's prompting.

He has led me to numerous resources and continues to
multiply and inspire my thoughts beyond what I would
have considered possible.

Secondly, as God has been *my* inspiration and enabler in
the writing of this book, so I believe that He may also be
saying to you its reader; that regardless of how
inadequate you may feel, or how often you have doubted
your ability to lead others in worship, He can use *you* to
facilitate worship and bring heaven to earth.

Instead of assuming that God will use someone who you
consider to be more 'spiritual' than you, I believe that He
wants you to understand that you can be the instrument
in His hand; the channel through which He can bless and
encourage others. You too can flow in His anointing and
draw people into His presence in worship. He's looking
for people who have a heart after His; a people whose
heart's desire is to worship Him in Spirit and in truth.

It's for You!

Some years ago when my wife Jo and I were Home-Group leaders, we relied heavily on the spiritual discernment of one of our co-leaders who seemed to have a hotline to God. As we met to prepare each meeting Lynne invariably received insights into needs within the group and, as new Christians, Jo and I tended to rely on her for guidance.

On one occasion she and her husband Philip were unable to meet for preparation. I remember thinking, 'That's it, we've lost our link with God! How are we going to know what He wants us to do at the next meeting?'

As Jo and I settled down to pray and listen to the Lord our level of expectancy was not particularly high. We hadn't been praying long when, to my surprise, I saw in my imagination a birthday cake being lowered into a room where my co-leader and I were sitting. I made no attempt to take the cake as I assumed that it was intended for her and not me. When we had finished praying, I telephoned another member of the group in order to try to clarify the meaning of this 'picture'.

She told me firmly, "It's obvious!" (It wasn't to me).

She explained that the cake represented God's gifts and that these were intended for me but I was unable to receive them because I had come to expect and rely on others to be the recipients of His gifts and revelations.

After this rebuke, Jo and I continued in prayer and waiting on the Lord. Our level of expectancy had now increased and God spoke to us with great clarity.

Who Me?

I have found it comforting to remind myself of the reactions of some of the Old Testament characters when God called them into His service; people like Moses, Jeremiah and Gideon. They were fearful and reluctant to obey God's call, considering themselves too weak and inadequate to carry out the particular task.

Joshua also must have been terrified at the prospect of succeeding Moses as the one responsible for leading the Israelites into the Promised Land. So much so that God had to reassure him 'Not to be afraid' no less than five times within the first nine verses of Joshua chapter one!

Yet, despite their self-doubt, God used them mightily. God isn't interested in a person's credentials or in their list of abilities and achievements, He looks at the heart.

Gideon was told by God that he had too many men for Him to deliver Midian into the hands of the Israelites, so He reduced Gideon's army from 32,000 to 300! (Judges Chapter 7:1-7). God gives His reasons for His actions in verse 2. He explains that He did this, *"In order that Israel may not boast against Me that her own strength has saved her."*

Gideon's strength and security were removed so that God would receive the glory. In his weakness, Gideon was forced to depend on God's enabling power to deliver him.

Confidence in our own strengths and abilities can hinder God's purposes, stunting our Christian growth and preventing us from entering into the fullness of all that He desires for us.

In fact God says that it's not the one who trusts in man who is blessed, but the one whose hope and confidence is in Him, (Jeremiah 17:5-8).

God isn't looking for the self-sufficient; those who have seemingly got it altogether, because they could be tempted to take the glory for themselves. Our God is a jealous God and He refuses to share His glory with anyone. He is not so much looking for our ability as our availability.

And, as testified to by Gideon and countless others through the ages, God's power is made perfect in weakness.

My prayer for you who believe that you are called to this ministry and who are prepared to make yourselves available to God, (regardless of your fears and perceived weaknesses), is that He will use this book as a resource to better equip and empower you for service; leading the people of God to offer up worship that is pleasing and acceptable to Him.

As those who are wearing 'L' plates, we have much to learn from others, and the information contained in this book has been gleaned from various sources: from Scripture, from theologians, from those involved in this ministry and much from my own experience. Whether you are someone who is tentatively considering entering this ministry or someone who has been involved in it for some time, I trust that this book will be of benefit to you, enabling you to develop your God-given ministry in service to Him.

My hope is that this book will be of help in alerting you to some of the pitfalls of the ministry of leading worship whilst affirming all that is good.

As we focus on the worship ministry we need to view it in the context of our Christian life as a whole.

When the seventy two returned after their mission, (Luke 10), reveling in the fact that even the demons submitted to them in Jesus' name, Jesus gave them some sober advice. He told them not to rejoice that the demons submitted to them, (that they had a 'deliverance' ministry), but to rejoice that their names were written in heaven.

The highest calling that God has on our lives is not to be pastors or worship leaders or to have any other type of ministry or title; it is to be sons and daughters of God. Jesus is reminding the disciples, and us, that our identity and security are to be found not in what we do but in who we are; sons and daughters of the living God. This is the safest and most secure platform from which to move out into ministry.

CHAPTER 2
Definitions Of Praise And Worship

When we *praise* God we declare truths *about* Him; about His character, about His works, about His divinity. Praise is the genuine response to God's love and goodness toward us and to His greatness. The more we become aware of who God is and all that He has done, the greater our response will be in praise of Him. Praise is central to true worship.

When we *worship* Him we begin to say things *to* Him with a greater sense of intimacy.

(I realise that worship should encompass the whole of our lives in that everything we do should reflect our worship to God. We honour Him and bring glory to Him when we conduct ourselves in Christ-like fashion, endeavouring to 'Be imitators of God' as Paul puts it in Ephesians 5:1-2. For the purpose of this book, however, when I use the term 'worship', I am generally referring to 'sung worship').

Praise - An Act of the Will
Admittedly there are times when our praise of God is simply a spontaneous outburst of gratitude in response to His manifest goodness or for His faithfulness in answering prayer.

At other times our praise can be triggered by a revelation of His being; a sudden awareness of God with us. But what about all those times when we just don't *feel* like praising Him; when the hustle and bustle of our busy lives cause us to feel less than joyful? Is it hypocritical to offer up praise to God when our emotions seem cold and detached?

The truth is that we don't have to *feel* like praising Him. Praise is not necessarily based on feelings; it usually starts with a conscious decision on our part to do it.

In Psalm 145 David says; *"I will exalt You, my God and King; I will praise Your name for ever and ever. Every day I will praise You and extol Your Name for ever and ever."* (v 1-2).

God is worthy of praise because He is God!

If we relied on our feelings as motivation to do something, then some of us would never get up in the morning! So as we decide to praise God, declaring truths about Him, we remind ourselves of His greatness, His power, His majesty, His faithfulness, His mercy, His love and His grace. As we focus our thoughts on Him in praise two things happen:

Firstly, we begin to lose sight of the cares of this world.

Secondly, we start to draw near to God.

His Word assures us that as we draw near to Him, He draws near to us (James 4:8). In fact He is always with us, His promise is that He will never leave us or forsake us.

But so often the cares of this world and our frantic activity cause us to lose sight of Him.

The God ordained pattern of worship that the Israelites adhered to under the Old Covenant involved a progression from the outer courts of the Temple via a sacrificial offering and the sprinkling of blood for the forgiveness of sins. The Priests were allowed to enter the Holy Place daily but access into the Most Holy Place, (or Holy of Holies), was reserved exclusively for the High Priest, and this only once a year on the Day of Atonement. The Most Holy Place contained the Ark of the Covenant, the symbol of God's presence. With the introduction of the New Covenant through the sacrifice and shed blood of Jesus, the Lamb of God, *"We have confidence to enter the Most Holy Place by the blood of Jesus, by a new and living way opened for us through the curtain, that is, His body."* (Hebrews 10:19-20).

As we continue in praise we become more aware of His presence, believing by faith that the way is open to the Father because of Christ's sacrifice, once for all. Instead of saying things about Him, we now want to say things to Him, to tell Him that we love Him, we adore Him. We bring our worship to Him. We have moved from the outer courts to the Most Holy Place, the place of intimacy with God.

Terry Virgo of New Frontiers International says this concerning worship:
"We can so easily fall short of God's best. Simply singing the most up-to-date new worship songs in pleasant succession is not the ultimate aim. We want to bring our personal and corporate devotion to God, to linger in His

15

presence and satisfy His heart with our love. In such a setting we should expect God to manifest Himself to us. He is our Father and we are His children, Christ is the Bridegroom and we are His Bride. The Holy Spirit is present wanting to make these realities 'come alive' to us so that we emerge having given God the glory due to His Name, and having received inner renewal and strength from Him."

In Psalm 100 verse 4-5 we are exhorted to,

Enter His gates with thanksgiving and His courts with praise; give thanks to Him and praise His Name. For the LORD is good and His love endures forever; His faithfulness continues through all generations.

Praising God with a grateful heart focusses our attention on Him and His goodness and prepares our hearts for more intimate worship.

We should avoid any tendency to restrict our praise and worship to a formula. Although the Tabernacle and Psalm 100 worship models may be helpful models to consider, let the Holy Spirit be the One Who ultimately directs you. Through Jesus we have entered into a personal relationship with God the Father and the key instruction given by Jesus is to worship Him in Spirit and in Truth.

There have been times when I have led worship when I sensed that the congregation were already in a place, spiritually, to enter into intimate worship. At times like this it 'just seems right' to sing more worshipful songs from the outset.

There's not a right or wrong way to lead worship as long as our heart's desire and motive is to bless God's heart.

CHAPTER 3

What Is The Basis Of Christian Worship?

Professor Paul Hoon emphasises that "The core of (Christian) worship is God acting to give His life to humanity and to bring humanity to partake of that Life. Christian worship is God's revelation of Himself in Jesus Christ and humanity's response." (*The Integrity of Christian Worship. Nashville: Abingdon Press, 1971*).

Here we have a summary of the Bible put simply; God wooing those He had created to the point of dying for them. God didn't sit back and wait for us to find Him, He was pro-active in revealing Himself to His creation. If ever we doubt that God wants to have a relationship with us, we need look no further than the cross in order to realise God's total commitment to us. God was in Christ reconciling the world to Himself, (2 Corinthians 5:19).

James F.White adds that, "It is a reciprocal relationship. God takes the initiative in addressing us through Jesus Christ and, we respond through Jesus Christ, using a variety of emotions, words, and actions." (*Introduction to Christian Worship, Abingdon Press*).

Note the words: "Using a variety of emotions....."

How can we truly worship God unless we use our emotions? It's impossible! (More of that later).

Before I became a Christian, I often wondered why it was that I was comfortable with someone talking about God, or The Church, or even Christianity, but not when they mentioned Jesus. The mention of Jesus always made me feel uncomfortable. I now realise that God, The Church and Christianity are all more general or impersonal terms and we can ignore them or reject them without our comfort being disturbed. Jesus, however, is personal. He disturbs our comfort and we cannot just ignore Him. He demands a response.

God said to Moses in Exodus 3:6, *"I am the God of your father, the God of Abraham, the God of Isaac and the God of Jacob."*. We do not worship some abstract, distant, irrelevant God. God is a personal God, a God of people Who has revealed Himself in Jesus in order that we might know Him and worship Him.

In his book, 'Worship', Evelyn Underhill begins with this statement: "Worship in all its grades and kinds, is the response of the creature to the eternal." (*Harper & Brothers, 1937*).

The way that we view God will affect the way that we worship Him. Selwyn Hughes explains that, "To think of God as uniquely other than everything in creation inspires adoration and worship. Without this idea in our minds, our worship is a mere ritual and a formality." (*source: www.allaboutgod.com*).

In order to worship God in truth we need to grasp something of the enormity of His being, His awesomeness, His power and His majesty. The fact that He is high and exalted. He is from everlasting to everlasting; there has never been a time when He did not exist, (Isaiah 40).

The writer of the letter to the Hebrews, having reminded his readers that they, (and we), are able to enter the Most Holy Place with confidence by the blood of Jesus, then exhorts them to *"Worship God acceptably with reverence and awe, for our God is a consuming fire"*. (Hebrews 12:28-29).

What The Bible Says About Worship
Worship is a High Calling.
King David set apart the priestly musicians for the responsibility of leading worship; they were released to do their work *'day and night'*. (1 Chronicles 9:33)

In Acts 6, the disciples were under pressure to get involved in the daily distribution of food to the widows of the Grecian Jews but they realised that if they did so they would neglect their calling to preach the Gospel and to give their attention to prayer.

Waiting on tables was obviously an important and necessary service but it wasn't what God had called them to do, so they delegated this task to others who were regarded as being more suited to this work. I wonder how many of us would have taken on this additional responsibility because we wouldn't want to let others down. In doing so we may have watered down the primary work that God had purposed for us and may have denied others who were better suited than us their opportunity to serve God and fulfil their calling. On closer examination of our motives perhaps we would have recognised that our response was prompted by guilt or trying to please man. To refrain from using our God given talents or to take on too many additional responsibilities may ultimately reduce the effectiveness of what God wants to accomplish through a body of believers.

This is not to suggest that we should consider ourselves above serving the Body when there is a need but that we should keep in mind God's primary calling on our lives.

Worship Restores Our Sense of Wonder

'For in Him all things were created: things in heaven and on earth, visible and invisible, whether thrones or powers or rulers or authorities; all things have been created through Him and for Him.' (Colossians 1:16)

We were created with an in-built capacity and desire to worship something greater than ourselves; namely God; creation worshipping its Creator. Worship restores our perception of how great and awesome God is. Even though He fills everything in every way, He becomes magnified in *our* eyes when we worship Him. And it's not that God is lacking in something and needs our worship, it's because *we* need it.

God Desires For Us to be Released in Our Worship.

In Exodus 9:1 the Lord said to Moses;

"Go to Pharaoh and say to him, 'This is what the Lord, the God of the Hebrews, says: "Let My people go, so that they may worship Me."

God is still calling out for His people today to be 'released' in order to worship Him freely. To be released from the bondage of fear of embarrassment; the fear of what others may think of us; the bondage of our culture that often resists any form of emotionalism in our expression of worship. To be released from tradition. Tradition is subtle and has the potential to hold us in bondage.

When Tradition Becomes Our Jailer
During the exodus, as Moses was leading the Israelites out of captivity, they came to Meribah but there was no water for the people to drink. The Israelites grumbled and Moses cried out to the Lord,

"What am I to do with these people? They are almost ready to stone me".

The Lord answered Moses, "Walk on ahead of the people. Take with you some of the elders of Israel and take in your hand the staff with which you struck the Nile and go. I will stand there before you by the rock at Horeb. Strike the rock, and water will come out of it for the people to drink." So Moses did this in the sight of the elders of Israel.' (Exodus 17:4-6).

Thirty-eight years later they came to the same place and again there was no water to drink. The people quarreled with Moses and started grumbling. Moses fell face down and the Lord said to him:

"Take the staff and you and your brother Aaron gather the assembly together. Speak to that rock before their eyes and it will pour out its water." So Moses took the staff from the Lord's presence just as He commanded him. He and Aaron

21

gathered the assembly together in front of the rock and Moses said to them, "Listen you rebels, must we bring you water out of this rock?" Then Moses raised his arm and struck the rock twice with his staff. Water gushed out, and the community and their livestock drank.(Num. 20:6-11).

But the Lord said to Moses and Aaron, "Because you did not trust in Me enough to honour what is holy in the sight of the Israelites, you will not bring this community into the land I give them." (v12).

Why was God angry with him? The first time God said, "***Strike*** **the rock**" and Moses obeyed. The second time God told Moses to "***Speak*** **to the rock**" but Moses relied on what had worked the first time and ***struck*** the rock. That's a reliance on tradition, not God.

There is nothing wrong with tradition providing that it is not binding, thus preventing us from seeing and being involved in the new thing that God is doing and denying ourselves the opportunity of being stretched in our faith.

The danger of tradition is that we, like Moses, can begin to take a pride in it, believing that we have the formula. Moses said, "***Must we bring you water out of this rock?***" God was denied the glory.

God was gracious and honoured Moses' actions but it wasn't His best for him. Moses missed out on entering the Promised Land, the place of fruitfulness and blessing. He elected to stay with the tried and tested formula; 'It worked last time, it will work again.' He heard what God said but chose not to risk failure before the watching nation of Israel.

The author, Somerset Maugham once wrote that, **"Tradition is a guide and not a jailer."** (The Summing Up, Doubleday, Doran & Co). In other words, we should draw from tradition what is good and helpful without becoming rigidly bound by it.

Jesus said, "Follow me!" The church is a movement not a monument and there is a need for relevancy and freshness in our worship.

Oppression In Any Form Can Hinder Free Worship. Psalm 137 relates an account of the Israelites who, during their captivity in Babylon, were asked to *'Sing one of the songs of Zion.'* Their captors demanded 'Songs of joy.' Their reply was, *"How can we sing the songs of the Lord while in a foreign land?"* (v3-4).

Compare the depressed emotional state of the Israelites during their captivity, to their joyful delight on their return to Zion, following their release. Psalm 126 verse 2 reads, *"Our mouths were filled with laughter, our tongues with songs of joy."*

Jesus came to set the captives free. He has rescued us from the dominion of darkness so that we too are free to worship Him with joyful abandonment.

Other Hindrances to Worshipping Freely
In an article that I was reading recently someone commented that he believes there is a "spirit of stiffness" in some churches! (Maybe a spirit of a *degree* of stiffness!)

I believe that many of us long to be more free in our worship; free to express our deep love and appreciation for all that God is and all that He has done.

Free to be ourselves, free to respond to God's great love for us, abandoned in glorious praise and worship of Him.

So, what holds us back from being more free in our expressions of thankfulness, praise and worship of God?

(Incidentally, what I am not saying is that there is something wrong with worshipping in silence in the quietness of our hearts. This is obviously valid and precious. But, when we hold back from expressing ourselves as we would really long to in our worship through fear of any kind, then we are not yet truly free).

Some may say that they *choose* not to be extrovert or enthusiastic in their worship, and that's fine, providing that their choice is based on freedom and not fear. We are only free to choose **not** to do something if we are free to choose **to** do it in the first place. For instance, let's take dancing in worship. I am only free to choose **not** to dance in worship if I am free to choose **to** dance if I wanted to. If my decision not to dance is based on fear; fear of embarrassment, fear of what others may think of me, fear of losing the respect of others, then I am not choosing from the basis of freedom but of fear.

God wants us to be free. *'It is for freedom that Christ has set us free.'* (Galatians 5:1).

What Else Prevents Us from Worshipping Freely?
Feelings of guilt and unworthiness. We don't *feel* worthy to enter God's presence; we don't *feel* that we have a right to be there.

The Bible declares that it's the knowledge of the truth that sets us free, not what we feel.

God has lavished His love on us and called us His children. We are sons and daughters of God; co-heirs with Jesus. The stunning truth is that God counted us worthy enough for Jesus to die for! We don't come in our own righteousness but in the righteousness of God which comes by faith in Christ; a belief in Who He is; *the* Son of God, and an assurance that through His death and resurrection He has freed us from our sins.

Our confidence to enter the Most Holy Place with boldness is based on what Jesus has accomplished by the shedding of His blood, (Heb. 10:19-21). Let the Word of God be the final authority in this matter and not your feelings.

Think of how Jesus willingly suffered and died for us. How can we doubt God's love for us or doubt His desire to fellowship with us. It was while we were still sinners that Christ died for us; the Righteous for the unrighteous, (Romans 5:8, 1 Peter 3:18). Jesus has prepared the way for us to come into the very throne room of Almighty God.

What an awesome God we serve and what a privilege to be able to worship Him freely and have opportunity to lead others in worship and adoration of Him.

In the next few chapters we will focus more on the priorities and practical aspects of the worship ministry.

CHAPTER 4

The Worship Group

Priorities in Worship

Where should our priorities lie in worship?

Graham Kendrick once made this observation concerning Christian worship. He says,

"It has for a long time been my conviction that whatever the methods or means employed in worship, however they may vary from Christian to Christian, or from church to church, the master key to worship is a revelation of the Lord in all His beauty. Such a vision will achieve in us a quality of worshipful response that no methodology, technique, composition (no matter how beautiful), choir, skilled instrumentalist or any kind of head knowledge could ever hope to arouse or sustain."

Worship of God has to be our priority and we must recognise that it is His initiative from beginning to end, both in the revelation of Himself in Christ and in the prompting of our response by His Holy Spirit.

Worshippers First - Musicians and Singers Second

During His temptations by the devil in the desert following His baptism by the Holy Spirit, Jesus was offered 'All the Kingdoms of the world' if He would bow down and worship Satan.

Jesus responded with words of Scripture, *"Worship the Lord your God, and serve Him only,"* (Luke 4:8). There we have it; **worship first, service second**.

I once heard the Canadian Bible teacher, Judson Cornwall, relate the following story. He said that his wife was one of those people who couldn't resist filling all the flat surfaces in their house with magazines, books and a host of other items.

Despite his pleading for her to tidy the litter, the problem remained. One morning, as he was leaving the house, he said to her, "Darling, I just want to tell you how much I love you and appreciate you. I am so pleased that I married you."

When he arrived home that evening, he was amazed to find that all the flat surfaces had been cleared of rubbish and the house had been cleaned throughout.

His wife's 'service' was in response to Judson's declared love for her. Our service too should flow out of our gratitude to God for His revealed love for us in Christ. Worship first, service second.

Although we are to be worshippers first and musicians and singers second, this does not imply that we should be careless or sloppy with our music, quite the reverse. God is deserving of our very best, the first fruits. Psalm 33 verse 3, exhorts us to 'Play skilfully'. In 1 Samuel chapter 16 verse 17, King Saul asked for 'Someone who plays well' to be brought to him. *We* are playing for the *King of kings,* so let's endeavour to play to the best of our ability. But, let us also be careful to keep in check the tendency to allow our music to become an end in itself, thereby replacing God as the object of our worship.

It is possible to get so wrapped up in debates and arguments concerning arrangements, style, technique or theory, that we can miss the point of why we are involved in this ministry: to worship God and to help others in their expression of worship to Him.

Lead by Example
If we are to lead others in worship then we are to be worshippers ourselves. We should not expect to take people to a place where we ourselves have not been. If you are not already doing so, then do try to make space during your rehearsal times to worship God yourselves.

In his book 'The Church in the Marketplace', the former Arch-Bishop of Canterbury, George Carey, relates this story:

'For some weeks, Chris and Suzie were undecided about their church commitment. We were still going through major disputes concerning worship and that kind of turbulence is enough to put anyone off going into the firing line.

But, eventually Chris took over the leadership of the music group, and it began to blossom.

This was simply due to Chris's conviction, shared and backed by myself, that the group had to be open to renewal itself before it could be a channel of change. "A music group is first and foremost a prayer group and only secondly a music group," he would repeat. And it is probably true that for the first year of Chris's year of office more time was spent by the group in sharing and praying than in actual music practice.

At first some of the group complained about the amount of time spent waiting upon God. "I came along to sing - not to pray," said one girl. Chris's reply was firm and courteous: "If you just want to sing, then go along to the choral society. But if you want to make an effective contribution to the music group you must learn that our role is central to the church's worship. We must be sensitive to the Spirit before we can be used by the Spirit."

This emphasis upon the group as a spiritual entity made an instant impact, not only upon individuals in the music group, but upon the congregation as well.

First, it led to an awareness in the music group that those engaged in any aspect of leadership in the church had to be open to God. And a quiet but important ministry started in the group. As they learned to share Spiritual experiences, and prayed and worked together, so the Holy Spirit led them into fresh experiences of His life and power. Some felt a deeper longing to enter more fully into the life of the Spirit. Through the laying-on of hands they were filled afresh with the Spirit's presence.

One girl who suffered from depression was healed through the support and prayer of the group.

A number received the gift of tongues which revolutionised their own spiritual lives, increasing their effectiveness in intercession. But this also led to a deepening appreciation within the congregation of the importance and power of music'.

(Used by kind permission of Lord Carey)

Be Filled With the Spirit

As this story highlights, if we are members of a worship group, then we too need to be open to renewal in order to be channels of change and we need to be sensitive to the Spirit before we can be used by the Spirit.

We are the body of Christ. In order for a body to exist and function effectively it needs breath. Therefore, as the body of Christ, we need the breath of Christ, His Holy Spirit.

When Jesus was sending out His disciples, (John 20 verses 21-22), He said, *"Peace be with you! As the Father has sent Me, so I am sending you." And with that He breathed on His disciples and said, "Receive the Holy Spirit."*

In our own strength we can only achieve so much, but God has made His Spirit available to us in order to empower and equip us to serve Him; ' "Not by might, nor by power, but by My Spirit" declares the Lord', (Zechariah 4:6). God's Holy Spirit is not an optional extra - He is our Christian life! The early Church came into being through the outpouring of the Holy Spirit at Pentecost, (Acts 2). Without Him there would be no Christian Church.

If Jesus needed the Holy Spirit before He could begin His earthly ministry, then how much more do we need Him.

Before the disciples began their ministry, after Jesus had risen from the dead, He told them to wait for the Holy Spirit who would endue them with power from on high. Having received this initial baptism in the Holy Spirit at Pentecost, they were again filled as they prayed together in Acts 4:31.

How essential it is for us also to be filled and refilled with the Holy Spirit, like those early disciples, if we are to be effective in carrying out God's will.

The Spirit of God is a good gift, (Luke 11:11-13). His Spirit fills us with power, love and self-control, (2 Timothy 1:7). **His Power** to enable us to do the works that He has called us to do; **His Love** to share with those who are lost and in need, and **His Self-control** to enable us to live a godly life in honour of Him. This is how we hallow the Name of our Father in heaven.

The Holy Spirit is the primary and essential requirement that we need if we are to continue the works of Jesus and extend His Kingdom here on earth.

Do you know the power of the Holy Spirit flowing through your life or are you operating in your own strength and feeling tired, weary, dry and ineffective? Just like the valley of dry bones in Ezekiel 37, we too can feel lifeless. But, with the Spirit of God breathed into our lives we can become a 'Vast army'.

Jesus assures us that our Heavenly Father will only give us good gifts.

He says, *"How much more will your Father in heaven give the Holy Spirit to those who ask Him,"* (Luke 11:13).

If you don't know personally this wonderful power that is available to you, then stop for a moment and ask God to fill you with His Holy Spirit. Ask Him to enable you to live the life that He wants you to live and do the works that He has called you to do. It is to His glory that you bear much fruit for Him, (John 15:8).

The Power of Music

I heard the story of a man who was lost in the jungle. It was getting dark, so he stopped to rest in a clearing. Suddenly a lion approached and prepared itself to attack. The man was petrified and froze. As the lion stalked towards him he frantically searched his pockets and found a penny whistle that he began to play. The lion heard the music and sat down to listen. A tiger, attracted by the music, walked into the clearing and was just about to pounce when he realised how beautiful the music was and sat down to listen. Next, a snake slithered into the clearing having heard the music and coiled itself ready to attack the man but it too appreciated the music and stopped to listen.

Within a short space of time many of the animals in the jungle were sitting in the clearing listening to the music as the man played his penny whistle for all he was worth.

Then suddenly, an elephant came into the clearing. He walked through the ring of animals up to the man, picked him up with his trunk and tossed him into the bushes. All the other animals came rushing up and asked him why he did that. The elephant replied, "Pardon?"

Music attracts! (Unless you're a deaf elephant that is!) However, our music should do more than just attract people into church, it should be a vehicle to draw them into the awareness of the presence and wonder of God.

In Psalm 27 the Psalmist is expressing his confidence in God,

"The Lord is my light and my salvation - whom shall I fear? The Lord is the stronghold of my life - of whom shall I be afraid."

Then in verse 4 he says,

"One thing I ask of the Lord, this is what I seek: that I may dwell in the house of the Lord all the days of my life, to gaze upon the beauty of the Lord and to seek Him in His Temple."

As those involved in leading worship, our responsibility is to give people a view of God as they follow our gaze. Therefore, it is important where we are gazing. Are we focussing on God in prayer, in reading His Word and in fellowship?

Verse 8 of Psalm 27 reads, *'My heart says of You, "Seek His face!" Your face, Lord, I will seek.'*

Like David we need to resolve to seek God's face with passion so that we can enter into the promise of Jeremiah 29:13, "You will seek Me and find Me when you seek Me with all your heart."

God is not interested in outward appearances of devotion, He looks at the heart, (Matthew 15:8).

Humility

A review of the priorities in this ministry reveals that:

1) we need to be worshippers first.

2) we need to be open to the renewing power of God's Holy Spirit in order that we may be transformed by Him.

3) we should endeavour to cultivate a close walk with God so that we act as sign-posts which point away from ourselves towards Him.

In addition to this, there needs to be humility in our approach and attitude to this ministry. Humility is not thinking less of ourselves but thinking of ourselves less.

Jesus has this to say concerning humility in Luke 14:8-11, *"When someone invites you to a wedding feast, do not take the place of honour, for a person more distinguished than you may have been invited. If so, then the host who invited both of you will come and say to you, 'Give this man your seat.' Then humiliated, you will have to take the least important place. But when you are invited, take the lowest place, so that when your host comes, he will say to you, 'Friend, move up to a better place.' Then you will be honoured in the presence of all your fellow guests. For everyone who exalts himself will be humbled, and he who humbles himself will be exalted."* (See also Proverbs 27:2, 25:6-7).

On one occasion, Simon Ponsonby, a former member of the church leadership team, gave some wise advice to the music group. He said, "The extent to which your ministry will prosper will be the extent to which you remain humble. Humility is to be the hallmark of your ministry."

It's advice that we have always taken seriously and been careful to heed.

In 1 Corinthians chapter 4 verse 7, Paul warns those who were becoming proud of their spirituality. He spoke this to them, *"For who makes you different than anyone else? What do you have that you did not receive? And if you did receive it, why do you boast as though you did not?"*

He goes on to say in 2 Corinthians 10:18, *"For it is not the one who commends himself who is approved, but the one whom the Lord commends."*

The following story has a serious message. A man fell asleep in his usual place on a commuter train. He would always wake just before the train pulled into his station. On this one occasion, however, the train stopped short of his station waiting for a signal to change. The man woke up with a start. He jumped up, grabbed his case, opened the carriage door, stepped out and fell onto the track. He quickly climbed back in again and dusted himself down as others looked on. As he shut the door, he said to his fellow passengers, "I suppose you think I'm really stupid for doing that!" He then walked across to the door on the other side of the carriage, opened it and fell out onto the embankment!

There's a warning here to any of us who think that we have "arrived" in this ministry; we can easily take a tumble. In any involvement in an "up front" ministry there is a danger that we can allow the plaudits of the crowd to take on more significance than is healthy.

Whilst it is encouraging to know that our ministry is

appreciated by, and helpful to those whom we are leading, we do need to beware of allowing pride to creep in with its tendency to steal the glory that rightfully belongs to God.

To the proud or to those who abuse His gifts God says; "I am the great I am. You are the great I'm not!"

When we fully understand the wonder of God's mercy and grace as demonstrated in Christ at Calvary, then humility should always be our response.

It was Isaac Watts' understanding of God's grace and provision and his resultant gratitude that inspired him to write this well-known hymn:

When I survey the wondrous cross
On which the Prince of Glory died,
My richest gain I count but loss,
And pour contempt on all my pride.

Forbid it Lord that I should boast,
Save in the death of Christ my God;
All the vain things that charm me most
I sacrifice them to His blood.
(Hymns and Spiritual Songs, 1707)

Be Alert to the Evil One's Tactics
Humility does not mean that we are to consider ourselves to be of little worth; after all God says that we are precious in His eyes and highly honoured, (Isaiah 43:4). Humility means that we resist promoting either ourselves or our agenda choosing instead to promote Him and His purposes.

We have a cunning adversary who seeks to undermine our position in Christ. He will accuse us of pride causing true humility to degenerate into a lack of self-worth.

I have often heard and sometimes entertained the accusations of the enemy when he whispers, "Who do you think you are to lead these people in worship, you're no more spiritual than they are, in fact.........". Then he goes on to remind me of all my failings.

This may happen whether you are leading in small groups or large gatherings. He will accuse you of being hypocritical, unworthy or proud. This is when, like Jesus in the wilderness, we need to wield the Sword of the Spirit, God's Word, to disarm our adversary. James 4:7 instructs us to submit ourselves to God, resist the devil and he will flee from us. We are to 'Take captive every thought to make it obedient to Christ' (2 Cor.10:5). In Revelations 12:11 we read that, 'They overcame him, (Satan), by the blood of the Lamb and by the word of their testimony'. Remind Satan that you belong to God; that you have been legally bought back by the shed blood of Christ. When the devil reminds you of your past, remind him of his future!

Unity
Psalm 133 (NLT).

¹ How wonderful and pleasant it is when brothers live together in harmony!
² For harmony is as precious as the anointing oil that was poured over Aaron's head, that ran down his beard and onto the border of his robe.

*³ Harmony is as refreshing as the dew from Mount Hermon
that falls on the mountains of Zion.
And there the LORD has pronounced His blessing,
even life everlasting.*

God blesses unity, not division. Without the unity that the Spirit brings in a group we are liable to lose God's anointing and end up ministering out of the flesh instead of in Spirit and in truth.

God desires to help us achieve this unity and harmony. Romans Chapter 15:5-7 reads:

⁵ May God, who gives this patience and encouragement, help you live in complete harmony with each other, as is fitting for followers of Christ Jesus. ⁶ Then all of you can join together with one voice, giving praise and glory to God, the Father of our Lord Jesus Christ. ⁷ Therefore, accept each other just as Christ has accepted you so that God will be given glory. (NLT).

Pray and ask God to help you, He is only too willing to respond.

It's important to note that it is not only with our mouths that we glorify God but with our hearts also. Our attitude towards each other and towards God is as important to God as the words that we sing. In Matthew 12:34, Jesus taught that 'Out of the overflow of the heart the mouth speaks.' He was quick to condemn the hypocrisy of the Pharisees for their outward show of righteousness whilst having hearts that were full of wickedness, (Matthew 23:27-28). 'Man looks at the outward appearance, but the Lord looks at the heart." (1 Samuel 16:7b).

John Wimber, himself a former musician with the sixties group "The Righteous Brothers", cautions that a professional background in music can sometimes be a negative factor.

He has observed that some with strong desires to 'make it' in music may need to go through a radical 'death' to success, in order to focus on God during worship and not be competitive. As Romans 15:7 directs we need to 'accept one another' and beware of competing with each other. Our attitude will determine our altitude.

Vision Statement

Let's move on now to more practical areas of this ministry and consider the usefulness of a group Vision Statement. First of all, do we need one? Secondly, what benefit is it?

A Vision Statement can be particularly helpful with regards to recruitment. Having a set of values in place when considering a candidate for a position in the worship group will assist you in making the right selection as well as making clear to the prospective member, from the outset, the aims and values of the group.

Here are some possible suggestions that you might consider including in a Vision Statement.

A) Recruitment

Should we allow anyone to become a member of the worship group?

One of the meanings of worship is 'to bow down and kiss'. We can only worship someone whom we really know.

We have to have knowledge of, and a relationship with that person. It follows, therefore, that it would be impossible to help lead others in worshipping a God who was not personally known to the one involved in leading.

Jesus said in John 3:3, that unless we are born again of the Spirit, we cannot see the kingdom of God. He tells the Samaritan woman at the well, (John 4:23), that God is Spirit and must be worshipped in Spirit and in truth, and in John 14:6 that He, Jesus, is the only way to the Father. In 1 Corinthians 2:14, Paul asserts that the man without the Spirit neither accepts, nor understands the things that come from the Spirit of God.

It is only through the Spirit of God that we can declare that Jesus is Lord. (1 Cor.12:3b). (See also Romans 8:9b: 'And if anyone does not have the Spirit of Christ, he does not belong to Christ.').

Accompanying worship is not just a matter of playing and singing well. If that were so, then with a certain amount of individual and corporate rehearsal, many musicians could become reasonably proficient at leading a group of people in singing hymns and choruses and gain a good deal of enjoyment and satisfaction in the process.

Worship is a Spiritual activity. Therefore in my opinion, only born again, Spirit filled Christians should be considered for this ministry. We need to be careful not to discourage enthusiastic enquirers but sensitively talk through the issues of Christian commitment and the need for a personal encounter with the living God whom we worship.

Whilst in the worship group at Holy Trinity Trendlewood, Mary produced the following mnemonic of worship:

W   Work together as a group to glorify God. Be united as a team.

"How good and pleasant it is when God's people live together in harmony". (Psalm 133).

O   Organise times of fellowship as well as regular practice.

Meet in each other's homes if possible (Acts 2).

R   Read your Bible to get to know God and to learn His will for you.

S   Skilfully use instruments and voices, (1 Chronicles 25 verses 7-8).

Although King David chose experts and trained musicians to minister in the temple, he also included the young, the old and beginners, (verse 8).

H   Honour God.

We are called to lead holy lives. We must be surrendered to God's will before we can lead others in worship.

I   In all that you do show His love.

Jesus commanded us to do this (John 13:34-35).

P   Pray together whenever you meet.

What Other Qualities Should We be Looking for in Prospective Candidates?

Here are some guidelines to consider. He or she should:

- have a heart for worship;

- be committed to God, group members and the church;

- be prepared to attend a number of rehearsals before being released into public ministry. This will confirm their commitment as well as allowing a probationary period for you and them to decide the suitability of their involvement;

- be teachable

A word about worship courses. They can be very profitable and we have certainly benefitted from them. But do beware of well-intentioned impositions to play or sing in a particular fashion. Having attended one such course we were so preoccupied in experimenting with different styles of playing our instruments and in creating more 'effective' arrangements that we were unaware of how unnatural our singing and playing had become.

After one service, I was asked by a church member if we were doing anything different in our leading of worship as she had found it difficult to worship for the past three weeks.

Let's all be open to improving our abilities and techniques but let us also be careful to avoid becoming so rigid or technical that we stifle our natural flair.

The Worship Group should:

1. Act as a signpost pointing to God.
2. Give a clear lead to the people.
3. Be joyful! Let your joy show in voices and faces.
4. Be open to the use of sequences of songs so that there is an unbroken flow of praise and worship
5. Be prepared to be silent when appropriate.
6. Plan prayerfully and be flexible.

B) Music Policy

It may be that in your church the leaders decide on the type of music that you are to play. If this is the case you may be restricted in your selection of music. But as servants and as those under authority, we all need to honour our leaders, although that should not deter us from discussing with them our views and preferences concerning worship.

If there is freedom to choose your music, then what type of music should you consider as being most helpful in the facilitating of worship in your particular setting?

Here are some thoughts for consideration:

What are the people used to? What is their experience? What can the church cope with? Not every song 'works' everywhere. For instance, a song that you may hear and enthuse over at a conference may not quite engage in the same way with the 10am church congregation on Sunday.

What can the musicians and singers cope with? Be willing to be stretched musically but know your limitations. We will always accompany best those songs with which we feel most comfortable and confident.

What form of music do you enjoy listening to and playing? What musical trends influence you most? In a large music group, there may be many and varied opinions concerning the type of music that should be used in worship. Whilst personal preferences may be expressed regarding the type of music that might be used, there should be a willingness to set aside our preferences, at times, for the overall good of the ministry.

C) Rehearsals

For various reasons, the frequency of practices will vary from group to group. At Holy Trinity Trendlewood church, the music group rehearsed once a week, on a Friday evening. The rehearsal lasted for approximately two hours and the main musical focus was usually the following Sunday's song list.

There are no fixed rules for rehearsals but within our practice times we have tried to implement certain priorities, although often we have failed to be as disciplined as we might have been in the outworking of them. We are still wearing 'L' plates! The following guidelines have proved of value to us and may help you decide what is right for you:

- Endeavour to put a time limit on your practice session.

- Try to be prompt and disciplined.

- Practice beginnings and endings, it inspires confidence.

- Make time for worship and prayer as a group.

- Learn to share together, opening yourselves to each other and to God. This may at first appear threatening but done in an environment of love, acceptance and confidentiality, it results in members growing in wholeness and bonding together in their concerns for each other. The effect on the group's worship ministry will be evident in its unity and harmony.

- Encourage laughter, it reduces stress and aids relaxation, that's official! In August 1985 the Royal College of General Practitioners issued the following statement: "Laughter affects every organ in the body. When we laugh, we secrete hormones that stimulate the heart and act as natural pain-killers. Stress is reduced, calories are burned off and digestion improved." The Bible also confirms that laughter is good medicine, (Proverbs 17:22).

- Practice linking songs together in order to facilitate flowing worship. An interesting idea is to link into the chorus of the following song.

- Think about songs that will flow together linked by mood, theme or key.

- Whilst it is important and often helpful to consider using songs that tie into the service theme, be open to selecting songs along an alternative theme, (providing that this meets with leadership approval).

- Again, with the service leader's permission, you might consider using songs creatively in conjunction with certain formal elements of the service. For example, during communion you could sing the song, *'It's your blood that cleanses me'*. Or, during the Offertory, *'This is my desire to honour You'*.

- Practice playing simple, well-known choruses without sheet music so as to aid spontaneity during worship.

- Consider including a short talk, a testimony or Bible discussion.

- If possible, distribute the list of songs to be rehearsed prior to the practice session in order to maximise the rehearsal time.

- Consider organising a Music Group 'Away day'.

Introduction of New Songs.
How Many?

At Holy Trinity Trendlewood we were blessed to have a number of church members selected and trained to lead services on a regular basis. Although their individual input brought great variety to our meetings, their diverse musical preferences sometimes put pressure on the music group when it came to learning the new songs that they chose. So much so, that we found it necessary to implement certain guidelines concerning the introduction of new material. We considered it unreasonable to be expected to learn more than two new songs within a practice session or to expect the congregation to cope with more than two unfamiliar songs during one service.

How Often?

With the wealth of Christian songwriting talent in evidence today, and with the prolific number of new songs available, it is difficult to know which songs to use and which to ignore. It is important to introduce fresh, Spirit-inspired songs into our worship, but the measure of how often we do this is in proportion to the congregation's ability to cope with them.

Whilst some can probably entertain two new songs in one meeting, to attempt this too regularly would be unrealistic. As well as putting pressure on them, it would prevent them from drawing the most out of each new song. Once a new song has been introduced, providing that it is not a 'one off' for a specific occasion, plan to feature it regularly for a period so that it will become more familiar to the congregation thus freeing them to focus on God and enter into worship. This after all is the goal of the worship ministry; facilitating intimacy with God.

The Music Group is Not a 'One Man Band'
Within a music group there will be various talents and giftings and it is important, as in any group of believers, to identify and encourage these gifts if we are to operate as a body and avoid a 'one man band' scenario.

We shall be looking at the profile of a worship leader in the following section, but what about the other members, how can they contribute?

Here are some of the gifts that we have identified in our own music group:

Administration, Organisation, Encouragement, Teaching, Listening, Discernment, Hospitality, Compassion and Prophecy.

It's helpful to promote an 'every member' input policy within the team whilst at the same time recognising that there needs to be an accountability to the group leader.

One helpful way to try and discern the gifts within the group is for members to ask themselves the following questions:

i) What do I enjoy doing?

ii) What do I think that I am good at?

iii) What do others say that I am good at?

As we celebrate the giftings of others within the group, we can encourage them and help them grow in their particular ministry. The gifts are God-given for the balanced functioning of the group and ultimately for His praise and glory.

CHAPTER 5

Worship Leading

Setting the Standard
The worship group has the opportunity to act as a role model for the church gathering in that it is able to display unity, humility and love, whilst focussing on God. When you consider that a river can only flow as high as its source then like-wise a congregation will seldom rise higher in its level of praise and worship than the level set by those leading worship.

Spirit and Truth
Jesus declared in John 4:23 that *"The true worshippers will worship the Father in Spirit and truth, for they are the kind of worshippers the Father seeks."*

In Spirit.
Forms and rituals in themselves do not produce worship. Worship is ignited within us only when the Spirit of God touches our human spirit. This is not to suggest that forms and rituals are not valid, it is simply to state that without the enlivening presence of the Holy Spirit they remain empty vessels.

In his book, *Whatever Happened to Worship?*, A.W.Tozer asserts that, "It is the operation of the Holy Spirit of God within us that enables us to worship God acceptably through that person we call Jesus Christ, Who is Himself God." *(WingSpread Publishers).*

In Truth

There needs to be integrity in our worship. To worship God with all of our hearts is to worship Him without pretence, *(Jeremiah 3:10)*. Jesus had strong words to say regarding the Pharisees' superficial form of worship:

"These people honour me with their lips, but their hearts are far from me. Their worship is a farce, for they teach man-made ideas as commands from God." *(Matthew 15:8-9 NLT).*

God is looking for more than just an outward show of affection, He's looking for worship that is heartfelt.

The Worship Leader

Why Have a Worship Leader?

If we are those who are to be led by the Holy Spirit as Jesus taught in John 16:13, and if we have been freed to serve God as a kingdom of priests, (Rev.1:6), why do we need someone else to lead us into the presence of God when we gather together corporately to worship Him?

Firstly, the book of Judges will help answer this question. When the Israelites were without a king to lead them, 'Everyone did as he saw fit', or as another translation reads, 'All the people did whatever seemed right in their own eyes' *(Judges 21:25 NLT).*

That's why God appointed Judges to lead and guide His people. The Worship Leader is one who is appointed to help give direction and maintain Godly order.

Secondly, as Christians we are all called to witness to the Good News, (Math.28:19,20), yet there are evangelists. We are all called to take care of others, (Galatians 6:2), yet there are pastors. We are all called to praise and worship God, therefore it follows that there will be those who are called and anointed as Worship Leaders.

What Are The Key Qualities of a Worship Leader?

The Worship Leader is to be a conduit, an artery carrying worship to the heart of God. If the artery is blocked, then the flow of blood is cut off and the body suffers. God has to be at the heart of our worship.

According to the teaching of the Rabbis, Satan was the heavenly worship leader of the angels until he became proud and desired to be worshipped himself, (Isaiah 14 & Ezekiel 28).

If the Worship Leader draws attention to his or herself rather than being the means of facilitating the worship of God, then God is robbed of His rightful worship and the body of Christ is also robbed of true worship.

Worship Leader Profile

A useful guide to the qualities to look for in a worship leader is as given by John Wimber in the following profile. Don't be put off if you fall short of the qualifications listed! Although some of these are mandatory, we should view the rest as standards to aim for with God's help and grace.

A. Character

1. A worship leader should be a long distance runner, not a sprinter. That is, he/she should be a person who is stable, committed and who has their personal life in order, (1 Tim 3:1-10, Titus 1:6-9).

2. He/she should perceive leadership as an obligation to service and self-sacrifice, rather than as a position or title to be used to exercise control or power or to command privileges or respect, (Mark 10:37, 42-45).

3. He/she should be a person of faith, filled with the Holy Spirit and wisdom, (Acts 6:3,5).

4. There should be a genuine love for people and for Jesus, without desire for personal benefit at the expense of the sheep, (John 21:17, Ezek. 34:1-10).

5. He/she must be a "team player", willing to help others succeed, (Philippians 2:3-4).

B. Musical Ability

1. It is helpful if the Worship Leader plays a "lead" instrument (e.g. guitar or piano), but not essential.

2. He/she must have a reasonably strong singing voice with good intonation.

3. A worship leader doesn't need to have a stage presence. In fact, he/she should be full of humility, willing to decrease and let Jesus increase, (John 3:30).

C. Anointing

1. When the person leads, does God come? That is does He respond to the worship? Are the person's prayers of invocation answered?

2. Is the person sensitive to the direction of the Spirit during worship?

3. Do the people follow and respond to the direction and flow of the worship?

4. Does the person often worship when he/she is alone?

Preparation for Leading Worship

Getting Ready for the Service.
How best can we use the time available prior to the service? Here are some suggestions:

A) Arrive in good time to set up equipment.

B) Check that instruments are in tune.

C) Always make time to pray! Remember that worship is a spiritual activity and we need the Holy Spirit to breathe on our offering and to anoint it.

D) Use time available to give attention to those songs that need another run through.

E) Ask God to release a spirit of expectation both within the music group and the congregation.

F) Ensure there is good eye contact between members.

Avoid concentrating on the practical to the exclusion of the spiritual. We bring to God in prayer all that we have prepared and leave it to Him to bless and multiply.

The Praise and Worship Time

The worship group needs to be sufficiently visible and audible to encourage the congregation in its worship without drawing overdue attention to itself; too loud and we will deafen them, too quiet and they will be self-conscious and tentative in their response.

Try to appear relaxed, smile and enjoy it. If you appear bored and disinterested your negative disposition will be picked up by the congregation and this could easily put a damper on the whole proceedings. Although we are not 'performers' in the worldly sense, we do need to communicate a sense of enthusiasm and joy, particularly during praise. The congregation will be looking to you not only to give a lead in music and song but also in attitude. Positive and negative attitudes are both infectious.

Fear and nervousness are two of the most common factors that inhibit freedom of expression in a meeting. If this is an area of concern for you, take it to the Lord in prayer. If you are a member of a music group, share your concerns with a group member and ask them to pray with you. It will be as much an encouragement to them to be asked to pray for you as it will be for you to receive prayer.

On God's Training Programme

Although I have had much experience in performing in pubs and clubs in the past, when I became a Christian I began to suffer from a very real, almost debil[...] nervousness that restricted my involvement in 'up-fr[...] roles. I remember calling out to God after 'shaking' wi[...] nerves yet again during the leading of worship in a service, asking Him to free me so that I would be released to be able to serve Him more effectively. Up to that point, I had only led a service on one occasion and that being some years before. Within a few days of praying this prayer I was asked if I would be prepared to lead a service in four weeks' time.

Common sense was urging me to say 'No' but deep down I knew that God was calling me to do it and I also knew that fear was no basis for refusal. (Let me just say at this point that there have been occasions when a request has seemed like a heavy burden being placed upon me and was without the accompanying conviction that God was in it. At these times I have learnt to say 'No'. Jesus said 'My burden is light and My yoke is easy'. In Acts 10:19-20 Peter received a clear witness from the Holy Spirit before he agreed to Cornelius's request to visit him).

But this was different. Although my stomach was in knots at the prospect, I was in no doubt that I was to agree to the request and trust God for His enabling power.

The next part of God's plan was equally as daunting. Within a few days of my agreeing to lead a service, I was approached by my sales manager and told that I would be leading a sales training course for my work colleagues. Standing up and speaking in front of the church was one thing but the thought of training my peers was just as scary a prospect for me at that time. What I wasn't aware of was that I was now on *God's* training programme!

r 13, the Lord tells Moses to send a
ach of the twelve tribes of Israel to
Land of Canaan and report back
and its people. Ten of the twelve
ᴏad report saying, "We can't attack those
ᴛhey are stronger than we are." "We seemed like
ᴜsshoppers in our own eyes, and we looked the same to
them." (vs 31 & 33) But Caleb and Joshua, who made up
the twelve, said this to the Israelite community, "Do not
be afraid of the people of the land, because we will
swallow them up. Their protection is gone, but the Lord is
with us. Do not be afraid of them." (14:9) In Deuteronomy
1:29, Moses recounts his words to the Israelites, "Do not
be terrified; do not be afraid of them. The Lord your God,
Who is going before you, will fight for you."

Ten of the twelve were focussing on themselves and the
circumstances, Caleb and Joshua were looking to the
Lord, trusting Him to give them victory over their
enemies.

God doesn't always remove the cause of our fear before
He leads us forward. How would we grow in faith if He
did so? But as we move forward in His will, trusting in His
promises and sovereign power, He drives out our enemies
before us and gives us the ground we claim.

This was exactly what God was doing in my own
circumstances. I had moved forward, trusting Him and
He was about to deal with my enemies.

On two occasions, prior to leading the sales training
course, God ministered to me, freeing me from fear of
judgment, fear of criticism and fear of embarrassment.

The night before I was due to lead the sales training meeting, I received prayer from a friend and God gave me a 'picture' that really encouraged me. In this 'picture' I saw myself entering the training room and God was sat with my colleagues proudly saying to them, "This is my son, listen to him."

Although I was still apprehensive and nervous before the meeting, as I walked into the room, I clearly sensed that God was sitting there just as revealed to me during the previous night's ministry. (His timing is perfect!) The peace of the Lord was truly with me and I was amazed at how relaxed I felt throughout the training session.

When I eventually led the service it was the same. Even though a member of the congregation collapsed during the service, I experienced the peace of God and was able to deal with the situation in a relaxed way. Although I was still nervous before the service, it wasn't the debilitating nervousness that I had experienced previously.

Worship and the Emotions

Should we be emotional in our worship? Yes, of course we should! God created our emotions and He operates through them. He doesn't by-pass them. How else are we to express ourselves except through our emotions! (Expressing our emotions is not the same as being ruled by them).

When we want to tell someone special that we love them we say it with feeling, with emotion, don't we?

Jesus was a man of emotions. He wept, He rejoiced, He anguished, He shouted, He expressed righteous anger.

The British culture is often resistant to any form of emotionalism in our worship, stiff upper lip and all that.

Many examples of the use of emotions are found in the Psalms. Psalm 95:1 for example:

"Come let us sing for joy to the Lord; let us <u>shout aloud</u> to the rock of our salvation". 'Shout aloud' actually means **shout aloud**! It doesn't mean sing quite loudly!

I was watching a rugby match on television recently and one side scored a try. I shouted, "Yes!" I nearly frightened the life out of my children. If we can get so excited about a game of rugby or football how much more should we get excited about God! 'He Who was without sin became sin for us so that we might become the righteousness of God', (2 Corinthians 5:21). A God Who loves and cares for us so much that He died for us, deserves our heartfelt praise and worship.

It was for freedom that Christ set us free! Freedom to show our love for Him through our emotions in response to His great love for us; a love that took Him from His place of majesty in heaven to the loneliness and pain of the cross at Calvary. A love that took Him to His death so that you and I might truly live.

But now He's alive! And I believe that the God Who has revealed Himself to us through His Word and through the earthly life of Jesus, wants to reveal Himself to us more and more in our worship and draw us by His Spirit to that place of intimacy with Him.

I mentioned earlier that we should aim to radiate joy and enthusiasm in our worship leading. But there will be times also when we need to be sensitive to the words that we are singing. A triumphal song, for instance, can be sung with gusto. Conversely, a song describing the sorrow and death of Christ would normally be sung more quietly and with feeling. Always attempt to convey the mood of the song by introducing 'light' and 'shade' into its interpretation.

A display of genuine, spontaneous emotion prompted by the Holy Spirit in our worship will be a powerful sign that God is in our midst, and far from this display of emotion having an adverse effect on the worship, it is more likely to lift it to a higher plane. Remember, a river can only flow as high as its source. When the worship group worships the people will be more encouraged to worship.

Not that we should consider ourselves to be failures if this is not our experience every time that we lead. For some time I had been concerned because I did not always feel 'spiritual' when leading worship. Was I being hypocritical in assuming the responsibility of leading others in worship? Should I consider stepping down? This was a very real issue as far as I was concerned because it challenged my conscience regarding worship in Spirit and truth.

My concerns were lessened after talking to a well-respected Christian musician and worship leader. He explained that when we lead worship we are carrying out our service to God and to His people. He went on to say that if we were in the seventh heaven each time that we led worship, then we would probably find it difficult to maintain contact with the congregation and may become self-indulgent.

Praise God there are times when we do experience the reality of God's presence in a special way but we can still be Spirit-led in our worship leading even though we may not always be lost in wonder, love and praise. We are those who walk by faith, confident that the One Who fills the heavens and the earth indwells us and is with us.

As a wise Christian friend of mine once said, "When the people find it difficult to worship when you are leading, then this is the time to be concerned."

The test of our calling to lead worship, therefore, is not whether we feel spiritual during the worship time but whether the people we are leading are able to worship. Is there an anointing on the worship? Does God come?

Worship that Flows

When the people arrive at the church or meeting some may be weighed down with various cares and concerns. For some it may simply be the normal hassle of getting themselves and their families to the meeting on time. For others there may be tensions in relationships or concerns about having to cook lunch, (if it's a morning service). Some may be distracted by family, health, financial or work concerns. For those carrying burdens of any kind, entering into intimate worship by just singing a song or two may not be easy. People need time to unburden themselves so that they can begin to focus on the One Who will carry their burdens for them. For most of us it takes time to move from the flesh to the spiritual. The "hymn sandwich" tends to create a 'stop-start' scenario, and is not always helpful in achieving this aim.

I heard the true account of a worship leader who had a

family history of heart conditions, namely hardening of the arteries. He decided to be pro-active in seeking the most effective type of exercise to combat this condition. After much research, he concluded that aerobics was by far the best method because it involved thirty minutes of unbroken exercise. God then spoke clearly to him using this analogy as a spiritual parallel concerning worship:

"Just as you need to exercise for thirty minutes to avoid hardening of the arteries, so I want you to exercise thirty minutes of worship to Me in order to soften your hearts."

We may not all be permitted the luxury of thirty minutes of sung worship during our services but I do believe that we should seriously consider the value of sustained periods of worship.

Freedom in Worship
It may be appropriate to encourage people to adopt a posture that is most comfortable for them as they praise and worship. It's not always necessary to stand. Although I am not a dancer, (ask my wife!), it's good to encourage people to feel free to dance.

I heard the story of a man who was asked by a fairly reserved member of his congregation why he danced when he worshipped God. He replied that it was because he couldn't fly!

On occasions it might be helpful to gently discourage the congregation from being concerned with the way that others are worshipping. Worship is unique and personal to each one and as such should be respected and not judged. Where we criticise and judge others with regards to their methods of worship, we run the risk of losing the sense of God's presence.

In 2 Samuel chapter 6, King David, 'Wearing a linen ephod, danced before the Lord with all his might', (v14), as he led the procession bringing the Ark of the Covenant back to Jerusalem. When Michal, David's wife, saw him 'Leaping and dancing before the Lord, she despised him in her heart', (v 16). On David's arrival home, Michal was cynical and rebuked him for the way in which he had expressed his gratitude to God. David replied, "It was before the Lord,...I will celebrate before the Lord." "I will become even more undignified than this, and I will be humiliated in my own eyes." (vs 21-22). The Ark was symbolic of the presence of God. David's joy could not be contained as he abandoned himself in the praise and worship of God, but his exuberance drew criticism from Michal. Her critical attitude and her disdain towards him had dire consequences. In verse 23, we read that she 'had no children to the day of her death.' Her critical attitude disqualified her from experiencing God's blessings.

A man went to see his doctor. Pressing his forefinger into his chest he said, "Doctor, when I press here it hurts." He then pressed his finger on his left leg and complained that this was also painful. It was the same when he pressed his neck and left arm. The doctor was rather concerned and puzzled and examined him thoroughly only to discover that he had a broken finger!

So often it's the finger that is pointing that needs healing. Could it be that the reason we criticise others is because their freedom makes us feel uncomfortable, challenging our lack of freedom?

Some years ago I attended a meeting in Birmingham where there was a mixture of denominations and cultures gathered together for praise and teaching. I had driven up in gale force winds and driving rain after a stressful day's work, and arrived with a thumping headache and feeling tired. Before the teaching there was an hour of praise and worship. During this time people were clapping and dancing, some were shouting whilst others were kneeling. Everybody seemed joyful except me! I was the odd one out. Their freedom was threatening to me and although I was envious of it, I found myself becoming critical of them in order to excuse and justify my lack of freedom. God convicted me of my sin and I confessed and received His forgiveness.

Although we may not feel comfortable with the style of worship exhibited by others, let's be careful that we do not fall into the sin of Michal, by standing in judgment of them. This is offensive to God and puts us at risk of missing out on His blessings whilst denying ourselves the wonder of His presence.

Isaiah warns against calling that which is good, evil, (Isaiah. 5:20). God looks at the heart and delights in worship that is offered in Spirit and in truth.

Run Your Own Race
The opposite of criticising others is the longing to be someone else rather than ourselves. If you won't be you, who is going to be you? God created you, chose you and called you by name to be you and not someone else. You are unique. You are precious in His eyes. God has an assignment specifically tailored to you, to your personality and to your giftings.

Comparing yourself to, or competing with others will only lead to pride on the one hand or discouragement on the other and prevent you from running the unique and particular race that God has set before you. (Hebrews 12:1)

We can also be inhibited or led to strive as a result of the unreasonable expectations that others put on us. God's burden is light and His yoke easy. May God free us from these false expectations of others so that we can be free to be ourselves.

This freedom to be ourselves should not be used as licence to do our own thing without regard for the feelings and preferences of those around us. We are part of the family of God and we should avoid any self-indulgent activity that disrupts our brother or sister's communion with God. I might enjoy raising my hands and jumping about during praise and worship but if in my enthusiasm I cause those around me to duck and dive, then I fail to consider the interests of others, (Philip 2:3).

Following After the Holy Spirit

It is sometimes appropriate during the worship time to give instructions to the gathering, as the Holy Spirit guides. In my experience, when the Holy Spirit prompts me to say or do something, He rarely does so with flashing lights. More often than not there is simply a feeling of rightness about a particular course of action. As someone once said: "You know it in your knower!"

In Acts 16:6-10, Paul had planned to visit Asia but was redirected by the Holy Spirit to Macedonia. We need to be willing to lay aside our plans if the Holy Spirit is leading us in a different direction. His way is best.

Personally, I'm not always comfortable with someone ordering me to praise and worship. (This is different from passionate exhortation. It's good to be passionate and enthusiastic). I believe that a congregation will respond far better to sensitive guidance and encouragement than to someone shouting at them. For example, during the worship we may sense it right to pause and suggest that the people offer thanks to God; quietly or out loud. Or we might encourage them to be quiet and allow the truth of the words just sung to sink in, taking hold of those truths for themselves. At other times we may be led to suggest a period of silence in order to simply enjoy the presence of the living God, allowing Him to minister to us at our point of need.

Although silence can be a helpful time to allow the congregation to experience the peace and love of God, for the one leading worship, it can seem anything but peaceful causing him or her to feel very exposed and uncomfortable. I know that at these times I have been able to relate to the person who said that he knew God was there but he just wished that He would cough now and then! For the one leading worship two or three minutes can seem like twenty. Be assured though that it will only seem like two or three to the congregation.

Bringing an end to the period of silence may be done by a prayer, a song or, where there is the freedom and permission to do so, inviting people to share anything that they believe God is saying to the church or to an individual. The latter will need to be in line with Scripture and in accordance with the guidelines as set out by your Leadership.

Helping people to worship by gentle encouragement and example is different from controlled emotional hype. Hype generally targets the emotions and operates out of the flesh. It is not necessary to 'work up' worship. We are those who walk by faith. In order to come to that place of intimacy with God, we need only to believe and trust that the sacrifice of Jesus on the cross was all sufficient to open up the way to the Father and enable us to enter the very throne room of God with boldness and confidence. Worship is our response to His love and grace; grace so amazingly demonstrated in the sending of His Son to die on a cross for our sins.

When I Lead Worship I'm Not Sure When to Speak or What to Say?

If this is a concern that you have then I hope that this next section will be of help to you. I have included it in direct response to being asked for help and guidance in what to say during a sung worship time.

The following suggestions may seem 'rehearsed' but can be beneficial in encouraging the people to focus on God whilst at the same time giving *you* confidence until such time that you are ready to rely on the Spirit to guide you. Having said this, it is not always necessary or appropriate to say much, or anything, during the worship time.

One of the aims in leading or facilitating worship is to create a flow that enables the people to engage with God. Sometimes spoken contributions help toward this aim, other times they can be a distraction. Pray and commit the worship time into God's hands, trust the anointing that is on you and, as you grow in your trust of the Holy Spirit's leading, seek to be sensitive to His promptings.

Introducing the Time of Worship

You may consider praying something similar to the following:

'Lord we acknowledge Your presence with us. Holy Spirit, we invite You to lead us and inspire us during this time. Breathe on our worship.'

Encourage the people to relax and to be expectant of encountering God's presence during worship. Remind them of God's promise that,

'As we draw near to Him He draws near to us,' (James 4:8)

You might describe some of the manifestations of His presence that the people could expect to experience. Here are some examples that you could select from to speak out:

- *In His presence we encounter His love that drives out all fear;*
- *His peace that passes understanding;*
- *His joy that strengthens us. He gives strength to the weary and increases the power of the weak.' (Isaiah 40:29) .*
- *In His presence we can experience His freedom – 'Where the Spirit of the Lord is there is Liberty!' (2 Corinthians 3:17).*
- *His Holy Spirit power is present to heal and set free. Be expectant to receive His healing touch today.*
- *Expect Him to speak to you in that place of intimacy. John 8:47 declares that, 'Whoever belongs to God hears what God says.'*

- *Allow Him to touch your hearts afresh with His goodness and love that follow you all the days of your life.*
- *You are His precious child and He wants to embrace you and reveal His Father heart toward you. He loves you as much as He loves Jesus. (John 17:23).*

You can use words or phrases of the song that you are about to sing. For example, if you are singing the song **'Come now is the time to worship'** by Brian Doerksen, here are some suggestions:

- *Thank You Lord that we can come before Your throne at any time to worship You freely, with boldness and with confidence. We have constant access to Your throne of Grace through the precious blood of Jesus shed for us.*
- *What an amazing privilege that we can come just as we are to worship You because of Jesus' sacrifice.*
- *Holy Spirit breathe on our worship. Lord Jesus we give our hearts to You today in worship.*

Or you can repeat some of the words or phrases from the song that you have just sung.

During the Worship Time
You can declare truths about God using Scripture verses or what you know to be true about Him from His Word. For example:

'Lord we praise You for:

- *Your goodness;*
- *Your faithfulness;*

- *Your mercy that endures forever;*
- *Your unfailing, unconditional love;*
- *Your compassion that never fails'*

(I have included a compilation of more of God's characteristics and attributes at the end of this section with Scripture references).

You might choose to declare that,

- *'God is here! He's present among us as we worship Him.'*

We can simply worship Him as we would on our own before Him. We can say things *to* Him in worship such as:

- *God You are awesome.*
- *Jesus Your Name is above every other name.*
- *Thank You Lord for Your love.*
- *Thank You for Your faithfulness that reaches to the skies and endures throughout all generations.*
- *Thank You Lord that Your Holy Spirit is here to help us in our worship.*
- *Thank You Father for lavishing Your love upon us and calling us Your children.*
- *You are good and Your mercy endures forever*
- *'Father/Jesus I love You, I worship You, I honour You and give You all the praise that's due Your Name.*
- *You deserve all the glory. You are holy, I praise Your holy Name.*
- *We lift our hearts to You today in worship. We come before You and bow at Your footstool in worship.*

Consider using helpful phrases to encourage people to praise and worship. For example, at the start of the praise and worship time you could encourage the people to lay aside anything that may be distracting them or weighing heavy on them and direct them to cast their cares onto the Lord because He cares for them. (1 Peter 5:7).

Here are some Scriptures that you may consider using or paraphrasing in your own words. (The book of Psalms is an excellent resource for this):

Psalm 8:1 *O LORD, our Lord, how majestic is Your Name in all the earth! You have set Your glory above the heavens.*

Psalm 33:1-3 *Sing joyfully to the Lord, you righteous; it is fitting for the upright to praise Him. Praise the Lord with the harp; make music to Him on the ten-stringed lyre. Sing to Him a new song; play skilfully and shout for joy.*

Psalm 29:2 *Ascribe to the LORD the glory due His Name; worship the LORD in the splendour of holiness.*

Psalm 59:16 *But I will sing of Your strength; I will sing aloud of Your steadfast love in the morning. For You have been to me a fortress and a refuge in the day of my distress.*

Psalm 63:3-4 *The heavens declare the glory of God, and the sky above proclaims His handiwork.*

Psalm 66:4 *All the earth worships You and sings praises to You; they sing praises to Your Name.*

Psalm 95: 1-3 *Come let us sing for joy to the Lord; let us shout aloud to the Rock of our salvation. Let us come before Him with thanksgiving and extol Him with music and song. For the Lord is the great God, the great King above all gods.*

Psalm 95:6 *Oh come, let us worship and bow down; let us kneel before the LORD, our Maker!*

Psalm 99:5 *Exalt the LORD our God; worship at His footstool! Holy is He!*

Psalm 100:4 *Enter His gates with thanksgiving, and His courts with praise! Give thanks to Him; bless His Name!*

Psalm 150 *Praise the LORD. Praise God in His sanctuary; praise Him in His mighty heavens. Praise Him for His acts of power; praise Him for His surpassing greatness. Praise Him with the sounding of the trumpet, praise Him with the harp and lyre, praise Him with timbrel and dancing, praise Him with the strings and pipe, praise Him with the clash of cymbals, praise Him with resounding cymbals. Let everything that has breath praise the LORD. Praise the LORD.*

Revelation 4:11 *Worthy are You, our Lord and God, to receive glory and honour and power, for You created all things, and by Your will they existed and were created.*

Here is a list of some of the characteristics and attributes of God that you can declare:

<u>God is</u>:

Love	1 John 4:16
Good	Psalm 100:5
Merciful	Ephesians 2:4
Faithful and True	Revelation 19:11
Unchanging	Hebrews 13:8
A Shield about Me	Psalm 3:3
An Ever Present Help	Psalm 46:1
A Father to the Fatherless	Psalm 68:5
The Good Shepherd	Psalm 23

God is (continued)...

The Lifter of Our Heads	Psalm 3:3
The King of kings	Revelation 19:16
The Lord of lords	Revelation 19:16
A Mighty Warrior	Zephaniah 3:17
The Alpha and Omega	Revelation 22:13
The Beginning and End	Revelation 22:13
The Great I Am	Exodus 3:14
The Ancient of Days	Daniel 7:13
The Only Wise God	Romans 16:27
The God of All Comfort	2 Corinthians 1:3-4
All Powerful	1 Chronicles 29:11
All Knowing	Psalm 139:3, Hebrews 4:13
Ever Present	Psalm 139:7-11
Holy	Revelation 4:8
Full of Grace and Truth	John 1:14
Compassionate	Psalm 145:8
For Us	Romans 8:31
Great	Psalm 95:3
Lord of All the Earth	Psalm 24:1
A Miracle Working God	Psalm 77:14
The Creator of All Things	Colossians 1:16
The Author of Salvation	Hebrews 5:9
The All Sufficient One	Genesis 17:1
Worthy of Praise	Psalm 145:3

He is:

My Shepherd	Psalm 23:1
My Delight	Psalm 43:4
My Friend	John 15:15
My Strong Deliverer	Psalm 140:7
My Protector	Psalm 91
My Refuge and Strength	Psalm 46:1

He is (continued)...

My Strong Tower	Proverbs 18:10
My Helper	Hebrews 13:6
My Father	Matthew 6:9-13
My Healer	Psalm 103:1-3
My Provider	Philippians 4:19
My Shelter	Psalm 91:1
My Hiding Place	Psalm 32:7
My Saviour	Psalm 68:19
My Hope	Psalm 71:5, Romans 15:13
My Righteousness	Isaiah 45:24
My Rock	Psalm 18:2
My Redeemer	Job 19:25
My Guide	Psalm 139:10
My Peace	Isaiah 9:6
My Joy Giver	John 15:11
My Restorer	Job 42:10
My Comforter	2 Corinthians 1:3-4
My Glory	Psalm 3:3
My Desire	Psalm 27:4
My Life	Deuteronomy 30:20

Inverted Pride

I have already mentioned the need for humility in this ministry and the dangers of pride; taking the credit and the glory for a "successful" worship time. But there is another equally subtle form of pride to beware of and that is 'inverted pride'.

There have been times when the praise and worship time has not gone as well as we would have liked. I remember one such occasion when we were invited to play at a midweek youth meeting in the church.

We were somewhat disorganised. We had forgotten to bring the acetates; our playing was not up to our usual standard; the equipment was problematic, and even though God was obviously present and touching people's lives, we were discouraged. Instead of celebrating what God was doing in our midst we were more focused on the negative aspects of our playing and accompaniment. The devil invited us to a pity party and we accepted the invitation! We discovered that God was teaching us a valuable lesson.

In effect our grumbling was a sign of inverted pride. What in fact we were saying through our despondency was that it is dependent on the way in which *we* perform that brings blessings on those whom we are leading and that the level of proficiency of *our* performance is what determines the level of God's blessing. This is inverted pride, assuming that *I* am responsible for the outcome. Pride and inverted pride both take the credit for the outcome of our performance, good or bad.

The reality is that God can bless people through us or in spite of us. Providing that we have prayerfully committed the time of praise and worship to God and have played to the best of our ability, seeking to make Him our focus, then we can leave the outcome to Him.

When we mistakenly assume the responsibility for that which is God's work, even though our motives are well intentioned, we take on a heavy and unnecessary burden. It is a lesson that I am still learning but this truth continues to be a source of liberation for me as I 'let go and let God'. I am learning to trust the anointing.

It was an encouragement to me when a friend told me about an actual woman who was known as Typhoid Mary. She was a carrier of Typhoid and she infected those with whom she came into contact without displaying the symptoms of Typhoid herself.

When we are called to lead others in worship we can be confident that we are anointed by God and that we carry His presence. It's His presence that will 'infect' those we minister to; whether we 'feel' His presence or not. So relax, set your heart on God and trust in His anointing to draw and inspire the people to worship.

CHAPTER 6

Worship In Small Groups

Many of the guidelines suggested in chapter 5 for the leading of worship in large gatherings will also be pertinent to small group worship leading. However, the dynamics of the small group are different to those of a public meeting and therefore require a slightly different approach in some areas.

How does it differ and what should be our approach to it?

i)   Relax, You're Among Friends

In comparison to the public meeting, the setting here is more intimate and often the leading will be more low key. There can sometimes be a tendency for the worship leader to feel more self-conscious within a small group setting as he or she is not physically set apart from the other members as would normally be the case during a church service. Don't be put off by this, other group members want to be led in their praise and worship of God and they will look to you, with appreciation, to help them.

ii) **Be Prepared Spiritually**

It is especially important in worship leading that, like King David, we keep short accounts of our failings before God. To lead worship in Spirit and in truth is difficult whilst harbouring resentment or unforgiveness, or deliberately indulging in sinful activity. Although we stand in the abundant grace of God and have already had our sins forgiven, (Colossians 3:13), if our hearts condemn us we do not have confidence before God and we may open a door for the enemy to accuse us and steal our confidence. (1 John 3:21).

iii) **Pray and Plan for the Worship Time**

As with any meeting, there should be prayerful planning and preparation. Consider selecting songs along a theme. For example you could concentrate on a characteristic of God: His love; His mercy; His power; His uniqueness; His faithfulness or His holiness. Or the songs could focus on His deeds and be thankful in their emphasis. Or they could illustrate the Fatherhood of God. You almost certainly will have suggestions of your own but these will give you some guidelines.

If you are using one guitar as accompaniment, then I would suggest that you select songs that you feel comfortable playing, especially if you are starting out in this ministry. It will help your confidence, and that is important in the early stages of development.

Try to avoid using songs that have numerous chord changes as this tends to spoil the fluency of the worship.

Usually in small groups the people will be seated and probably a little self-conscious in their singing due to the more intimate setting. Both of these factors can inhibit them with regard to 'hitting' the high notes.

How many times in small groups have you witnessed magnificent attempts at reaching the high notes often ending up in hilarious laughter? It may even have been you! (or me!) I'm sure that God understands, He looks at the heart - we have to listen to the noise!

To avoid this scenario I will either choose songs with a lower register or continue to use the songs that I feel led to include and transpose the key downwards. On the odd occasion I have tuned my guitar down a tone where the featured songs have included uncomfortably high notes.

iv) The Worship Time

a) Be Flexible

Having planned the musical content and direction of the worship time, be ready to 'alter course' if necessary. If the people arrive tired and weary, it may not be appropriate to start with the rousing praise choruses that you have selected. Be sensitive to where the members are emotionally, spiritually and physically. They may well respond better to more gentle thanksgiving songs, therefore it is a good idea to include one or two additional choruses in your planning so as to accommodate this possibility.

b) **Hearing from God**

Although the small group can inhibit vociferous praise, its intimate atmosphere provides for a safe place to share and to be open to the Lord.

As the worship time progresses and the people are being drawn closer to God, endeavour to make space for Him to speak to the group, sharing what is on His heart. If this is uncharted territory for you, then the prospect of leading this 'quiet time' may cause you to feel anxious. So, how can you best prepare for this in such a way as to reduce those very real fears without assuming such control as to deny God room to speak and move?

Whilst we can never tie God down to a formula, (God cannot be boxed), having some guidelines in place when planning a time of silence will remove many of the fears of stepping out into the unknown. The following suggestions may be of help:

Advise the group members before the singing that there will be time given to wait on the Lord following the worship, or introduce it just preceding the time of quiet. Explain that this is not a time for prayer but for listening to God. It may be that you want to encourage them to speak out any revelation from God as it is received, or wait for the quiet period to finish before they share. Clear instructions from you at this point will help to eliminate any confusion.

It may be helpful to give examples of how God has communicated to His people in various ways throughout biblical times. For instance through:

i) **A word of knowledge**; for example to Ananias, (Acts 9:11), to Peter, (Acts 10:19,20) or

ii) **A symbolic picture**; given to the prophet Jeremiah, (Jeremiah 1:11-16).

One possible method of entering the quiet time could be by way of a song, such as *'Open our eyes Lord, we want to see Jesus'*, or *'Open the eyes of my heart, Lord, Open the eyes of my heart, I want to see You'*.

In order to help people relax during the time of silence, advise them beforehand of the time that will be allowed for waiting; for example 'five minutes'. Explain that you will bring the time to a close so that there will be no need for anyone to occasionally open one eye to see if they are the only one still with their eyes closed!

If the sharing out of this time is to take place after the waiting rather than during it, I have found it more productive to encourage each member in turn to share rather than to ask for volunteers. The latter method can lead to awkward silences or result in only the more outgoing of the group sharing. Often it is the more reserved in the group who will have the most valuable contribution to make.

We should be careful that we do not put anyone under pressure when trying to draw out what God may have revealed to them. Use gently probing questions such as; "What do you feel that God was saying to you during the waiting time?" or "Did you sense God impressing something on you during this time?"

If there is a reluctance to share, never push, give people time to review and maybe suggest that they can share later if they wish.

Encourage members to share any thought that came to them during the waiting time, no matter how obscure or insignificant that it may have seemed to them. Often what appears silly to one person can speak powerfully to another.

When leading a home group some years ago, my wife and I were preparing for a meeting, waiting on the Lord and seeking to know if there was any need that He wanted to meet during the meeting. As we waited, I received a 'picture' in my imagination of a gold block above me with a screw about to be hammered up into it. I was immediately aware that to use a hammer would result in bending or breaking the screw. Although not out loud, I shouted, "The screw must be gently screwed into the gold block with a screwdriver not hit with a hammer!" A screwdriver appeared and began to turn the screw. As it did so, gold dust showered down from it. What a strange picture and what was its meaning?

As we prayed about the picture, we believed that God wanted to show someone in the group that He desired to take them deeper into Him and pour out His blessings on them. Through the picture He was reassuring them that He would do this in a gentle way. After a further time of waiting on the Lord we sensed God indicate clearly the actual group member for whom the picture was intended. (This person was usually very reluctant to receive prayer and we were a little apprehensive concerning his reaction).

During the meeting we shared the picture and offered the possibility that God wanted to minister to this individual. (When presenting a word or picture believed to be from God it is always wise to offer it as a possibility in case we have misheard or its origin was not of God).

To our surprise, the person received it and permitted us to pray for him. He shared afterwards that God had spoken to him through the picture that we had presented, removing his fear and dealing with his reservations concerning receiving prayer.

As a result of our obedience in sharing a seemingly obscure picture, God prepared the way for that person to be the recipient of a wonderful blessing. God is so good!

If a person shares a word or picture that doesn't appear to make sense to you, don't panic! Ask if any other members of the group have the interpretation; you may be the one leading but you don't have to have all the answers.

c) **Who's in Charge?**

Are we prepared to let God be God in our meetings? It's risky but if we truly desire for Him to be Lord, then that means Lord of our lives and circumstances - meetings included! When God is present in our worship anything could happen and we need to be ready to drop our agenda in favour of His. His agenda is infinitely better!

God may disturb our comfort, but when He is allowed to break into our meetings we can be assured that it is in order to accomplish something of greater eternal value. His will and His work are perfect.

CHAPTER 7

Sons And Daughters Of God

'Therefore, there is now no condemnation for those who are in Christ Jesus, [2] *because through Christ Jesus the law of the Spirit who gives life has set you free from the law of sin and death.' (Romans 8:1-2).*

At the beginning of this book I emphasised the importance of ministering out of the security of knowing that we are sons and daughters of the Living God, and I believe that to consider this further is a fitting way to begin to bring things to a conclusion.

The Apostle John declared in 1 John 4:16, *"And we have known and believed the love God has for us."*

The Father's overwhelming desire for us is that **we know and believe the love that He has for us**, (1 John 4:16). He wants us to be absolutely convinced that the barrier of sin has been removed by the sacrificial death of His Son, Jesus, and to be in no doubt that we are accepted in the Beloved. There *is* now no more condemnation!

'Therefore, since we have been justified [that is, acquitted of sin, declared blameless before God] by faith, [let us grasp the fact that] we have peace with God [and the joy of reconciliation with Him] through our Lord Jesus Christ (the Messiah, the Anointed).' (Romans 5:1 Amplified Bible).

God has removed the penalty *and* the guilt of sin and declared us righteous through Christ's atoning sacrifice – Jesus took the punishment that brought us peace with the Father... *'He was pierced for our transgressions, He was crushed for our iniquities; the punishment that brought us peace was on Him, and by His wounds we are healed.'* (Isaiah 53:5).

It's all by God's grace! We had nothing to do with it. God wasn't even on our radar when He put His plan of redemption into place.

[4] ...Because of His great love for us, God, who is rich in mercy, [5] made us alive with Christ even when we were dead in transgressions....[8] For it is by grace you have been saved, through faith—and this is not from yourselves, it is the gift of God— [9] not by works, so that no one can boast. (Ephesians 2:4, 5, 8 & 9).

The Father initiated this reconciliation for one reason and one reason only – *'Because of His great love for us.'* **He loved us!** And the Good News is that we receive this new life and restored relationship with Him through faith; *simply by trusting in Jesus' once–for-all, perfect sacrifice on the cross of Calvary. It's a total work of grace but we receive the benefits by faith.*

A New Identity

We now have a new identity in Christ. We are no longer the same people that we were before we believed in Jesus. We are born again from above; born of the Holy Spirit. We are in the world but not of it.

We are new creations in Christ – the old has gone, the new has come. We are adopted into God's family - He calls us His sons and daughters. The Apostle John marvels at this in 1 John 3:1 when he declares:
'How great is the love the Father has lavished on us that we should be called children of God, And that is what we are!'

We are co-heirs with Jesus; loved unconditionally; righteous. (In Romans 5:17 the Apostle Paul states that: *'We have received the abundance of Grace and the gift of righteousness.'* – It's a GIFT!)

We are forgiven; seated in heavenly places far above all rule and authority; holy and dearly loved by the Father; chosen & called by name; blessed – redeemed from the curse; friends of God; precious and honoured in the Father's sight. We are invited and encouraged to call the Father 'Abba' – Daddy!

And yet how often do we read John 3:16 with the following unspoken sentiment: *'For God so loved the world that He gave His one and only Son...(Terms and Conditions apply!)'* If we are honest, that's how some of us subconsciously filter Scriptures concerning the Father's love for us. "He loves me when I do good and if I don't do bad; He loves me when I'm lovely and get it all right. He loves me when I meet all the terms and conditions."

The truth is that Jesus has already met all the terms and conditions on our behalf, (Romans 8:4, 10:4), and in Him we can now have total assurance of the Father's love. There are no disclaimers in the small print; no 'Ifs' or 'Buts'; no strings attached. He loves us unconditionally, (without conditions), because He chose to and nothing we do, or don't do, can separate us from His love!

In his classic work, '**The Pursuit of Holiness**' Jerry Bridges says this concerning the Father's love:
"*God's unfailing love for us is an objective fact affirmed over and over in the Scriptures. It is true whether we believe it or not. Our doubts do not destroy God's love, nor does our faith create it. It originates in the very nature of God, who is love, and flows to us through our union with His beloved Son.*" (Navpress)

What Hinders Us from Knowing the Father's Love?

The main stumbling block to our relationship with the Father is that, somewhere along the line, we have believed a lie concerning His unconditional love, His goodness, faithfulness and kindness.

God's original plan, (before sin came into the world), was that our earthly fathers should represent Him in demonstrating unconditional love to us and imparting identity, significance and purpose into our lives. His intention was also that we should have confidence in our earthly fathers' desire and ability to protect and provide for us.

Because of sin in the world and the absence of perfect role models in their own childhood, our earthly fathers were only able to do this imperfectly at best.

And so our perception of God as Father has been coloured to one degree or another by our own experience of being fathered.

How Can We Know the Truth About the Father?

If we want to know what the Father is really like we need only look at Jesus. He is the exact representation of the Father's being, (Hebrews. 1:3). He revealed the true nature of the Father in both His words and His actions.

Jesus told Philip *'If you've seen Me you've seen the Father.' (John 14:9)*. He said that He only did what He saw the Father doing and only spoke the words that the Father gave Him to say, (John 5:19 & 12:49). That's why Jesus calls Himself the Truth; and it's in knowing the Truth that we are set free to live our lives in the knowledge and security of the Father's love for us.

You might want to take a moment to ask the Holy Spirit to show you if there are any lies that you have believed about the Father and then pray the following prayer:

'Father God, thank you for revealing Yourself to me in Jesus. I repent of believing any lie that casts doubt on Your love, goodness and kindness toward me. I choose to believe that Jesus perfectly demonstrated Your heart, Your character, Your compassion and Your unfailing love and goodness. Now I ask, dear Father, that you reveal Yourself to me as I seek to know You more fully through the life and ministry of Jesus. Please make Yourself more fully known to me and through me. I ask this in Jesus' name. **Amen.***'*

(For more understanding of the Father's unconditional love I recommend visiting: www.encounteringthefatherslove.org)

CHAPTER 8

Worship and the Overflow

Jeremy Sinnott, former Senior Associate Pastor of the Toronto Vineyard, defines worship in this way:

"Worship is a personal and intimate meeting with God in which we praise, magnify, and glorify Him for His person and actions. It is the act of freely giving love to God. We meet God and He meets us."
(Main Street Mystics: The Toronto Blessing and Reviving Pentecostalism. Margaret M. Poloma. Published by Rowman Altamira).

An encounter with the living God during our worship will revive us and change us.

The people of Israel had the right motive for wanting to be revived. In Psalm 85 verse 6 we read: *'Will You not revive us again, that Your people may rejoice in You.'* They wanted to be revived in order to rejoice in God, to enjoy Him. They desired to know again the joy of the Lord. When we experience the joy of the Lord we are strengthened! Nehemiah 8:10 states that; *'The joy of the Lord is your strength.'* When God revives us there is joy and that joy is our strength.

Have you noticed how much more energy we seem to have when we are doing something that we enjoy, and how we rise above the circumstances and view problems from a different perspective when there is joy in our lives. This supernatural joy is released into our lives as we worship God.

We Worship Him Because He is Worthy

As we spend time in His presence we are revived, strengthened and encouraged through His joy. *'Splendour and majesty are before Him; strength and joy in His dwelling place'* (1 Chron. 16:27).

And this was the testimony of the writer of Psalm 16:11; *'In Your presence is fullness of joy!'*

The overflow of this encounter will be a renewed desire, enthusiasm and boldness to witness to others concerning the grace and love of God.

In Acts chapter 4, Peter and John were brought before the rulers, elders and teachers of the law because they were teaching about Jesus and His resurrection, and because they had healed a crippled beggar in the Name of Jesus.

This was the observation of those officials, *'When they saw the courage of Peter and John and realised that they were unschooled, ordinary men, they were astonished and **they took note that these men had been with Jesus!'** (v13).*

The disciples' joy and enthusiasm was so great because they had spent time with Jesus. They couldn't help speaking about what they had seen and heard, (v20).

As we come together expectantly, believing that Jesus desires to meet with us, throwing off the things that entangle, just as David threw off his kingly robes, we are released to worship God and to bless Him through the inspiration of the Holy Spirit. In this interaction, God blesses us so that we can be a blessing to others.

Always, the glory belongs to Him.

ABOUT THE AUTHOR

Martin worked for several years as a professional singer and musician before becoming a Christian, whereupon God harnessed his natural talents for the encouragement and enabling of the Church in worship. He has wide experience of leading worship, both in small groups and larger gatherings, and is acknowledged as an anointed worship leader, sensitive to the Holy Spirit and bringing a strong sense of the presence of God.

www.calledtoworship.co.uk

Printed in Great Britain
by Amazon

37351193R00061